Keltic Knots for Kids

Kathy O'Meara

Perelandra
Design

This small (5x8) book contains 17 drawings of Keltic Knotwork inspired by the Book of Kells. These animals and symbols are geared to appeal to younger children.

Books by Kathy O'Meara

Keltic Crosses Coloring
Keltic Crosses Coloring 2
Keltic Alphabet Coloring: Capital Letters
Keltic Alphabet Coloring: Lower Case Letters
Keltic Coloring: Knots & Numbers
Keltic Coloring: Knotted Nature
Keltic Alphabet Coloring 2: Capital Letters
Keltic Alphabet Coloring 2: Lower Case Letters
Keltic Creatures For Kids
Keltic Knots For Kids

Stained Glass "Window" Patterns
Spring Flowers
Summer Flowers
Autumn
Circle of Life
Keltic Christian

International Standard Book Number

ISBN-13: 978-1727105087
ISBN-10: 1727105087

DRAGON

FOX

SPIRALS

2 CATS

BUTTERFLIES

SCROLL

CRANE

STARS

EAGLE

HAWK

SHAMROCK

BUTTERFLIES

CAT

HEARTS

SPIRALS

DRAGON

DOG

TREE OF LIFE

2 SALMON

www.ingramcontent.com/pod-product-compliance
Lightning Source LLC
Chambersburg PA
CBHW061325250726

48657CB00003B/1041